# YOU KEEP
# ON PUTTING
### IT OFF
# BEING SAVED

# YOU KEEP
# ON PUTTING
## IT OFF
# BEING SAVED

## BREN DANIELS

# YOU KEEP ON PUTTING IT OFF BEING SAVED

*iUniverse books may be ordered through booksellers or by contacting:*

*iUniverse*
*1663 Liberty Drive*
*Bloomington, IN 47403*
*www.iuniverse.com*
*844-349-9409*

*Because of the dynamic nature of the Internet, any web addresses or links contained in this book may have changed since publication and may no longer be valid. The views expressed in this work are solely those of the author and do not necessarily reflect the views of the publisher, and the publisher hereby disclaims any responsibility for them.*

*Any people depicted in stock imagery provided by Getty Images are models, and such images are being used for illustrative purposes only. Certain stock imagery © Getty Images.*

*ISBN: 978-1-6632-2141-4 (sc)*
*ISBN: 978-1-6632-2164-3 (hc)*
*ISBN: 978-1-6632-2142-1 (e)*

*Library of Congress Control Number: 2021907654*

*Print information available on the last page.*

*iUniverse rev. date: 04/26/2021*

# IT'S EITHER
# HEAVEN OR HELL
# MAKE YOUR CHOICE

# GOD IS

# SOON

# TO COME

This Book is an Inspirational book to encourage you. For you not to wait until it's too late to get save.

Hebrews 3:7 Wherefore as the Ho'ly Ghost saith. Today if ye will hear his voice.

Hebrew 3:8 Harden not your hearts, as in the provocation, in the day of temptation in the wilderness.

# Contents

## Being Saved

## Change

## Choice

## Complete

## Decision

## Eternity

## Heaven

## Hell

## Help

## Hope

## Love

## Praying

## Reaping

## Salvation

## Serving The Lord

## Time

## Trouble

# 1

## You Keep On Putting It Off (Being Saved)

You go around saying I'm going to get saved. But you keep on putting it off.

You say I will before I leave this world. You keep on putting it off.

How do you know when your going to leave this world? This could be your last day.

You keep on putting it off. This could be the last words you read. Quit putting being saved off. Before it's to late.

# 2

## Why Do You Keep Putting Off Being Saved

Look back over your life. Haven't God been good to you. When you needed provision didn't he provide. When you needed help wasn't he there for you. And when you felt lonely didn't that feeling leave also. So why do you keep putting off being saved.

Even though you're not saved you know yourself someone had to help you out of the things you have been through. And came out of it was God that delivered you. So quit putting off being saved. So you can be free today.

# 3

## Today Salvation Has Come To You

Today salvation has come to you. Don't turn aside and neglect to serve me. For I am the truth. For I am the way the truth and the light. I can be your bright morning star. I can give you hope where you may fill there is no hope. Salvation has come to you. Don't turn away. You have another chance before it's too late.

# 4

## *When You Get Saved You Should Know Longer Be In Darkness*

———— ❊ ————

When you get saved. God brings you out of darkness into his marvelous light. You are no longer in darkness. Your eyes come open to the truth. The devil can't bind you up like he use too. Because God will give you power in his word. To help you when the devil comes to mess with you. God will bring up his word. That's why you must read God word. So you want be in darkness. For God word will keep you in the light. So to stay out of darkness. You must read. God word for the rest of your life.

# 5

## There's Nothing Bored About Being Saved

Some people have been saved for years. And they are bored are act bored about serving God. God takes you from glory to glory. So, what's wrong with the people who are bored. If it's you examine yourself. And see if this fits you. Do you pray? Do you fast? Do you stay before God presence. That will make you glad. In God presence is fullness of joy. If this doesn't fit you. Then that's why you have lost your joy.

*6*

## Saved And Loving It

I am Saved and I love it. It's the best thing I could have ever done. Was to except Jesus as my Lord and Saviour. I feel great. I feel good. I have peace. I have joy. I have love. I have strength. I am settle, I am stablish. I am doing fine. I love to serve Jesus and he is mine. I love my salvation. For Jesus is truly mine. And I love being saved and I am doing fine.

# *If You Die With Jesus Paradise Awaits You*

If you leave this world and you have accepted Jesus Christ as your Lord and Saviour. Paradise awaits you. The thief on the cross told Jesus. Lord remember me when thou comest into thy kingdom. Jesus said unto him. Verily I say unto thee. Today shalt thou be with me in paradise. Jesus has the power to say where you go. Base on your choosing. And what you say.

# *With Jesus In Your Life You Can't Lose*

When Jesus is in your life you can't lose. No matter what battle you face it is a fixed fight. Jesus went to Calvary for you and me. To save us. And when you are his child nothing you go through. He want be there with you. Troubles do come but they don't last always. Just like it rain sometimes later the sun comes out. Just like trials come but they also pass. So you can't lose. Because battles you face they are not yours when you belong to God. They are God's battles. That's why he says the battle it's not yours, but God's.

# Being A Child Of God

Being a child of God. You will never be alone. For God says I will never leave you are ever forsake you. You have protection. You have a healer. You have a deliver. You have everything you need. God takes good care of his children. Psalm says I have been young, and now am old; yet have I not seen the righteous forsaken, nor his seed begging bread. God will take care of you when you belong to him. When you are young he will take care of you. And when you are old he will still take care of you. God takes care of his own.

# 10

## *There Are Benefits In Serving God*

When we serve God. He wants us to be blessed. He blesses us every day in some way. Psalm says Blessed be the Lord, who daily loadeth us with benefits, even the God of our salvation. God blesses us every day we wake up. If you woke up this morning your blessed. If you have food to eat your blessed. If you have a place to sleep your blessed. If you have someone to love you. You are blessed. Just serving God your blessed.

# *What's It Going To Take For You To Change*

Don't let it be too late for you to get right with God. You know not the day nor the hour. That your life will be over. It's good to live free of burden. Especially when you know you are saved. And that way you don't have to worry. That if something happen if you're going to be alright. You don't have to worry if you die. Were you are going. If you get saved why things are alright. You don't have to wait for something to happen. For you to make a change. Because you might wait to late. And it's over for you. Because you waited to late before you made a change.

# 12

## We Didn't Come Here To Stay

<hr/>

We didn't come here to stay. We are just passing through. That's why as we age. Our body begins to change. Things that didn't use to bother us began to bother us. Like running. You may still run but not like you use to when you were younger. Your face may begin to change. You may not look like you use to when you were a teenager. You have signs that let you know things are changing. And we are just passing through. So as you see the change right before your eyes. You need to decide where you will be after this life. Because you will spend somewhere in eternity. That decision is up to you.

## 13

### How Come You Still Want Serve The Lord

❋

You still keep going through and you still don't know what to do. You have tried so many things nothing seems to work. Still you want let God help you. If you allow God to come in. He will change you within and he will be a friend. If you will let God come in.

## 14

### You Said I'm Going Too Do It One Day

You keep saying one day I will get saved. You keep putting tomorrow off. For what you can do today. Who says you're going to be here another day. You don't know neither do I. So don't keep putting salvation off for another day. I pray you don't wait until it's too late.

# 15

## Who Do You Have Your Mind On

What you yield your members too. That's were your mind is at. Whatever you do that's were your heart is at. If going to the clubs, selling drugs. Getting tied up in the wrong things. That's were your mind is at. Whether it's worldly are whether it's Godly. What you yield your members too. That's what you got your mind on.

# Do You Fear God

If you fear God you are careful what you do. Because you know God sees everything you do. You will treat people right. And you will do what's right. Because you know God is watching you, both day and night. So look at yourself and see if your careful what you do. And then you will know if you really fear God. By the things you do.

# 17

## Why Put Off Another Time What You Can Do Today

Why put off being saved to next Sunday. Are another time. How do you know you will be around. Tomorrow is not promise to you. Neither is it promise to me. So don't put off being saved tomorrow. What you can do today. Because who is to say you will be here another day. Only God knows what day and what hour. Only he can say what will happen tomorrow.

# You Will Never Be Ready

People say I will get saved one day. But I'm not ready. You will never be ready. For the devil will tell you, you are not. He wants you to stay in darkness and not to come in light. Know man can come to God except he draws them. You will never be ready for the devil will say no. But, tell the devil you're going to get saved know matter what it feels like. God can save you and he can fix you. To get you ready for heaven. For he knows the time is near. So you can just say yes no matter what it feels like. Are no matter what you have done. But if you're feeling you're not ready. The devil has already won in your life. And that's what he wants.

# God Is Not Willing Any Man Should Perish

God is not willing any man should perish. But, that all should come to repentance. So we are not going to have an excuse at judgement day. This is for the people that are not saved. God gives us a choice and that is true. So it's up to use to make the choice if we want to serve him too. God want everyone to be saved. But he gives us all a choice. And that will show were we end up on the day of judgment day.

# God Gives Us A Choice

God give us all a choice. Where we are going to spend eternal life. The choice you make will show by your life. You live the way you make your choice. And that determine where you are going. You don't have to stay were you are going. If you live in sin, you must know there's a judgment at the end. And you will pay for all of your sins. So make the right choice and live. For one day you will be judged according to the way you live.

## 21

### *You Have A Choice To Make*

You have a choice to make will you serve God or not. The choice is yours. Joshua says but as for me and my house, we will serve the LORD. Will you and your house serve the LORD. It is up to you. It can take one person in the family to get saved. And stand in the gap for other loved ones to get saved. Will you be the one. The choice is up to you. Will you be the light in your family. The choice is yours.

# 22

## Jesus Is A Gentlemen

Jesus is a perfect gentlemen. He will not force himself on you. In Revelation says Behold, I stand at the door, and knock: if any man hear my voice, and open the door, I will come in to him, and will sup with him, and he with me. You have to open the door for him to come in. He will not enforce himself on you. You have to open the door. Just like a gentlemen will open the car door for someone. You have to open the door to let Jesus in. For Jesus is a perfect gentlemen.

# 23

## There Is Completeness With Jesus

Jesus will be everything you need. He will complete you. If you have a void in your life an emptiness that just not filled nor can be filled. It's JESUS that's missing in your life. If you haven't excepted him in your life as your Saviour. That's the part of your life that will always be empty. Jesus will complete your life. When he comes into your life he complete you.

Matthew says But seek ye first the kingdom of God, and his righteousness; and all these things shall be added unto you.

# 24

## Jesus Is The Answer

Jesus is the answer for whatever you are going through. There is no problem that God cannot solve. God is a problem solver. A miracle worker, a great healer, a mighty deliver, a way maker, a promise keeper. Jeremiah say Behold, I am the LORD, the God of all flesh: is there anything too hard for me? God is asking a question? Give him a case. And I guarantee he can work it out. There is no problem God cannot solve.

# Do It Like God Say

If God give you something to do. You better do it like God say
to do, are something will happen to you. Remember Nadab
and Abihu the sons of Aaron. In Leviticus the 10 Chapter
and 2nd verse. When they offered strange fire before the Lord,
which he commanded them not. And there went out fire from
the Lord and devoured them, and they died before the Lord.
So do it just like God say are you will regret it later. For when
obeying God you will have success at the end. So do it like
God say and you will be victorious to the end.

## One Day For Salvation Came But One Day Was Too Late

You went to Church the Pastor called an altar call. For those who don't know the Lord. And for those who was lost. You didn't move an inch knowing you felt something pulling you to go from deep down within. But you didn't move an inch. Then you walked outside to get in your car. A truck was coming down the street. And you didn't see it. You got hit from the truck. And guess what you died and you were lost. So don't let this be you. When you can easy be saved and that wouldn't be you. For if you were to get hit by a truck. And you had given your life to Jesus. You would go to heaven and your soul wouldn't be lost.

# 27

## *Don't Let The Devil Talk You Out Your Blessings*

———※———

You may hear many voices speaking to you. But if the one you're listening too. Doesn't line up with the word of God. Then be careful who you are listening too. That's why it's important to read the word of God. God word says my sheep know my voice and a stranger he will not follow. So read God word so when you hear voices talking to you. You will know if it's God. Because God will speak to you thru his word. And you will never be deceived when voices is talking to you. And you want let the devil make you miss your blessing when he start talking to you.

# Don't Let The Devil Tell You To Say No To God

You sometimes say, no to this and say no to that. But one person you should never say no too and that's God. God will always be there for you. He will pick you up when you're feeling down. He knows just what to do. In whatever situation you may be facing. So, don't tell him no tell the devil no. And when he start trying to tell you to do wrong. Say devil I say no to you.

# Stop Letting The Devil Lie To You

You get put in a situation sometimes. You may not have money so you go into the store. Knowing if you steal something you're going to jail. You sell drugs knowing if you get caught you going to spend years in jail. Are you can smoke drugs, but you want get addicted. But yet you do it anyway. You need to quit letting the devil lie to you. When he says it's okay to steal you want get caught. Are it is okay to sell drugs you're just going to do it until you get what you need. He want ever tell you the truth. He makes it look good. On the outside, but he know what your end will be. He knows the wages of sin is death. So quit letting the devil lie to you. For there's no truth in what he is telling you.

# Today Is The Right Day

—❈—

Today is the right day to witness. Every day is the right day to give hope. Any day can be a right day. To tell people that Jesus is the one who saves. So, tell people it's time to get it right with God. Any day can be the right day. But today is the day. To get saved for today is the right day. And you are blessed that you woke up another day.

# The LORD Drawing You But You Keep Rejecting Him

God keep drawing you, but you keep rejecting him. You hear a soft voice say it's time to get saved. But you don't want to give up the things you are doing today. You know what your doing is wrong. That's why you don't want to get saved. For you know you have to give up your ways. But it's so easy to do what's right. So, don't keep rejecting God. For he keep drawing you. Because one day you may be excepting him and it's too late.

# Ask God What To Do

When you don't know what to do. Ask God what to do. He will show you what is right. God will never lead you wrong. Ask God what to do. And he will guide your life. It's God who knows what to do. So ask him in prayer what to do. And in prayer he will show you what to do. So you will make the right decisions. So you will know what to do. And what you do. You want regret it later. For God will show you what to do.

# 33

## *Some People Think Time Waits For Them*

———※———

Time waits for no one. Tomorrow is not promise to know one. The word of God says Today if ye will hear his voice, harden not your hearts, as in the provocation. You see tomorrow is not promise that's why you need to surrender your heart. While the blood is running warm in your veins. For if you die in your sin. The Bible says were I am you cannot come. Don't wait until it's too late. For time waits for no one.

# 34

## *Time Waits For No One*

Time should be precious to us all. Because it waits for or on no one. There is a time to be born and a time to die. We don't know when our time has come to an end. But one thing is for sure. That is an appointment that we all will meet one day. That is why it's so important to know Jesus. Because when that time comes. And one day it will come. You will see it's nothing wrong with leaving this world when you're going to be with Jesus. It's a blessing

## 35

### You Can Be Gone In A Minute

Who's to say you will be here in the next minute. In an instance you can be gone into eternity. That's why the word say if the Lord will, we shall live, and do this, or that.

We can make our plans. But it's in God hands if we are here to carry them out. So we don't know what tomorrow holds. But I do know God is in control of every minute. And we don't know how much time we have here on this earth. But God does.

# 36

## Where Will You Spend Eternity

You will spend eternity somewhere. You are either going to Heaven to be with the LORD. Are you going to Hell. There is an eternity and you chose were your destination will be. Romans talks about That if thou shalt confess with thy mouth the Lord Je'sus, and shalt believe in thine heart that God hath raised him from the dead, thou shalt be saved. And Luke talks about the rich man that went to hell. He said I pray thee therefore, father that thou wouldest send him to my father's house. For he said I have five brethren; that he may testify unto them, lest they come into this place of torment. Hell is a place of torment and you will be there throughout all eternity.

# Where Will You Go After This Life

You make the decision. The choice is up to you what you do. You see God is a good God. And he gives us free will. He will not enforce himself on you. He give you the choice. So whatever you choose. The choice is up to you. Where you go after this life. You are the one who choose. God has left that up to you.

# There Is A After Life When You Leave This World

Many people may feel they are living for the now. Not considering after this life. There is an eternity. You see God put everyone on this earth for a purpose. We are not just here. After our time is up here. The way we live our life in this world. Determines were we spend eternity after this world. Ecclesiastes Say To everything there is a season, and a time to every purpose under the heaven: A time to be born, and a time to die. Where will you spend eternity? Where will you go after this life?

# Lord What Is It That You Will Have Me To Do Today

Lord what is it that you will have me to do today. To do your will is what I love. To go forth in you and tell your word. I adore you I worship you. I praise you and adore you. I love to share you with others. I love to tell of your love. I love to tell of your goodness. You are the love of my life. You are the joy of my strength. I love, worship, and praise you. You are my love.

40

# You Should Be Excited About Your Salvation

—❋—

How come you don't witness. I don't understand why? You can see someone going thru and know they need help. But you never mention I can help. Neither do you mention my name. Where is the excitement you should have for representing my name? Where is the excitement you had when you first got saved? Now you act like you don't know me. You don't even mention my name. You still should be excited about serving me. If you say you're saved and you are serving me. I am God and I am still the same. So start back telling people about me and that I can still save.

# God Has Always Been Here For Us

God has always been here for us. If you still are living this apply to all of us. God has showed mercy even when we wasn't living for him. He cared for us when we were in sin. We should love him with everything within us. Especially for him saving us. So if you are not saved think about this poem and give him your life today. Just to know he has been here when we all know, that all of us has sinned and come short of the glory of God. So even thou we have sinned he has still been good to us. And God has always been near for all of us.

# 42

## It Was God Who Was Your Lawyer

───◦❈◦───

You may have had to go to court. Didn't know how it was going to turn out. You were worried within knowing you didn't have the money to pay. But God brought you out. And you know it wasn't you. Because you didn't have to put up a fight. The battle is not yours it's the Lord. So, let God be your lawyer, doctor, finance provider, protector. And you will always come out on top. For God can bring you out. No matter what you face in this life.

# 43

## The Battle Is Not Yours It's The Lord

You may be faced in a test and you don't know what to say are what to do. But hold your peace and let God fight for you. The battle is not yours it's the Lord. God will give you what to say. And he will stand up for you. So let God fight for you. For it's not your battle it's the Lord. So, let him fight for you. And he will stand up in you. And he will bring you thru. For it's his battle and not yours.

# 44

## You Have Help When You Serve God

You are never alone when you serve God. People may walk out on you. Betray you, misuse you, abandon you. Let you down. But when you have the LORD on your side you have help. God can make ways were you see no ways. God can give you favor when you have no money. God can open doors that you thought was impossible to open. When you are down and feeling blue. Just remember the God you serve. Is right there to help you.

## 45

# The Lord Has Been Good To All Of Us

God has been good to all of us. Yes, you and yes me even when we were lost in sin. He was still good to us and he treated us with kindness anyway. We all should be thankful to God for what he has done for us. Throughout the years we have lived on earth and still do. And to take his love and kindness for granted shouldn't be. For whether you are saved are not. God has still been good to all of us.

# God Has Compassion On Us

God says in his word he has compassion on whom he will. God has been very patient with us. Long suffering, gentle, kind, faithful, even thou we wasn't kind. He has been good to us even when we wasn't good to him. He has been compassionate to us. Even when we were living in sin. So now that you are saved you should have compassion on others. Because of the love God has showed to us. We should have compassion for others.

# God Has Been Merciful To Us

God word say he has mercy on whom he will. God has been merciful to us. He has been kind he has showed love even thou we wasn't serving him. He loved us when we were in sin. He has been good to us and still is. So be merciful to your neighbors. And be kind because God has been faithful and merciful to us even when we wasn't saved. It's God who brought us out by his grace. And because he is merciful to us. We need to show the same mercy to others every day.

# 48

## God Keeps Giving You Second Chances

God is a God of second chances. But yet you keep rejecting so great salvation. Living right gives you peace within. You don't have to be burden within. If you let Jesus guide you. You will always win. So as God give you a second chance take it and win. If you were in a car accident and God spared your life. You may have had a disease and God healed you. You may have had a stroke and God delivered you. God gave you a second chance and you know. So get it right and take the chance God has given you. And get it right. And live for God for the rest of your life.

# Jesus The Writer

Jesus is the writer for ever book I write. It's God who gets the glory each and every day. I can only write if the Lord lead me too. It's my Jesus who gives me wisdom to write as I do. So don't look at me and think it's me. Because God gets all the glory and not me.

# 50

## The World We Live In

In this world there will be heartache and pain. But there will also be good days as well. We just have to balance the scale. And trust God know matter what we go through in this world. We have to trust God even when we can't trace God. But remember he said he will never leave us or every forsake us. He would be with us even until the end of the world. So keep your faith in God. In the good times as well as bad. Because whatever you are going through it's working for your good.

# 51

## Jesus Can Make Your Life Beautiful

Jesus can make your life beautiful when you give it to him. Yes things will come up in your life. But just knowing you have Jesus on your side. You can handle it because you are not alone. Jesus can turn the rough places into smooth places. Jesus can turn your mountain into hills. Jesus can make all the crooked places straight. Jesus can make your life beautiful. Because he is in full control. And he is in control of whatever you fill that is controlling you.

# 52

## God Is Good All The Time

God is good all the time. Even when things are not going right. He is still good. You may not understand why you are going through certain things. But later on down the road. You will understand it by and by. You see God has planned know defeats for our life only to give us an expected in. Jeremiah says For I know the thoughts that I think toward you, saith the LORD, thoughts of peace, and not of evil, to give you an expected end. God's thought toward you are for good. For he is good all the time.

# 53

## *It Was God Who Was Your Healer*

———— ❊ ————

God was your healer. He was your doctor. Whatever you needed to be healed of. God is the one who brought you out. No matter if it was cancer, sugar diabetes, toe fungus, headaches. Whatever the problem may have been. God can be your healer each time you need him. So stay saved and continue to pray. So when you need God to come thru for you. You will know he will always be there always.

# God Can Heal You

God can heal your broken heart and bind up all your wounds. God can heal any sickness, disease, heartache, pain. God can heal your brokenness. You just have to give it to him and believe he can. It's according to your faith. You have to believe when you come to God. He can do what you are asking him to do by faith. Because there nothing that God can't heal you from. He is the great physician. You just have to believe he can.

## Your Either One Step From Heaven

Your either one step from heaven. When we leave this world. This is not the end. There is a Heaven and we are either going or not. The word talks about it in Revelation And I saw a new heaven and a new earth: The word lets you know heaven is there. You can either live for God and let your eternity be in heaven with God. The choice is yours. Where you spend your eternity it's up to you.

# Heaven Is For Real

Heaven is a beautiful place. John talks about In my Father's house are many mansions: if it were not so, I would have told you. I go to prepare a place for you. Heaven is already prepared for those who want to go. And you cannot go without Jesus. Jesus is your way to Heaven. You have to accept him into your life to get to Heaven. He is the way.

# There Is A Place Called Heaven

God said I am Alpha and Omega the beginning and the end. God is in heaven a place prepared for a prepared people. You have to live right to go to heaven. Anybody just can't go to heaven. You got to want to go to heaven. It starts by the way you live here on earth. The way you live tells your story where you want to go. Just like people purchase insurance just in case something happen. You serve God here on earth. So if you leave this world. You already know where your home is. 2 Corinthians. Say We are confident, I say, and willing rather to be absent from the body, and to be present with the Lord.

# Heaven Was Created For Those Who Except Jesus Christ As There Lord And Saviour

~ ❈ ~

Yes, you have to be saved to go to heaven. Romans says That if thou shalt confess with thy mouth the Lord Jesus, and shalt believe in thine heart that God hath raised him from the dead, thou shalt be saved. You have to except Jesus Christ as your Lord and Saviour to go to heaven. Heaven is a prepared place for a prepared people. That is why you have to except Jesus as your Lord and Saviour. You are preparing yourself for heaven.

# If You Die In Your Sins You're Going To Hell

The word of God says. If you die in your sins were I am you cannot come. That's what God word says. If you live hard on earth. Why do you want to go to hell? Hell is a real place and that is true. God tells you about hell even in his word. So get saved and live for Christ. For if you die in your sins. You have lost your chance for eternal life.

## Your Either One Step From Hell

Hell is a real place. And if you don't except Jesus Christ as your Lord and Saviour. You cannot go to heaven. The Bible talks about in Luke The beggar that died and was carried by angels into Abraham's bosom. And also the rich man that died and was buried. And in hell he lift up his eyes.

# 61

## Hell Is For Real

The Bible talks about in Isaiah how hell hath enlarged herself and opened her mouth without measure; You see there is room for anyone who don't know Jesus Christ in the pardon of their sins. If you don't know Jesus and you leave this world without him. There are only two places that you can go. Either Heaven or Hell. You have that choice. Hell is for real.

# 62

## There Is A Place Called Hell

───◦❋◦───

The rich man in the Bible lets you clearly see hell is real. It's nothing wrong with being rich. Just don't let the riches have you. Don't look down on the poor. But be a blessing to them if you can. The beggar only desired to be fed with the crumbs which fell from the rich man table. But he wouldn't even help him. And when the beggar died he was carried by angels into Abraham bosom. But when the rich man died he went to hell. He even wanted Abraham to let Lazarus the beggar. Come that he may dip the tip of his finger in water, and cool my tongue; for I am tormented in this flame. Then he said I have five brethren that he may testify unto them lest they also come into this place of torment. Hell is a real place.

# 63

## Hell Was Not Created For Mankind

⟶ ❈ ⟵

Hell was created Matthew talks about for the devil and his angels. You see God don't want us to too go to hell. He wants us to live right. Treat people right. Help people when we can. Do the right thing. And love your neighbor as you love yourself. Do unto others as you would have them do unto you. Because God says if you die in you sin. Where I am you cannot come. Don't leave this world without Jesus as your Saviour.

# 64

## Success Comes From God

Success comes from God. It's God who can put you on top. You don't have to do it yourself. God says if you humble yourself he will exalt you. So success comes from God. Promotion doesn't come from the east are the west. But promotion comes from God. So, let God give you success and he will give you the best. And there's nothing that people try to do. They can't take your success.

# 65

## Who Are You Going To For Help

Who are you going to for help. A counselor, lawyer, doctor, supervisor. Have you went to Jesus? Jesus can help you in every area of your life. Seek God for help and he will bring you out. It's nothing wrong with going to man. But, go to God first for he it is that can bring you out. So, go to God for help and not man. For there's nothing to hard for God to fix. For he is not man.

66

# God Can Deliver You

God can deliver you from whatever have you bound. God can make it lose you and let you go. Sickness knows the name of Jesus. Poverty knows the name of Jesus, etc. Philippians Says That at the name of Je'-sus every knee should bow, of things in heaven, and things in earth, and things under the earth. Everything has to come in line when Jesus speaks. So whatever you need delivering from. Call on Jesus. He will deliver you.

# 67

## God Can Keep You Mind

God can keep you in perfect peace if you keep your mind stayed on him. There will be many things that come up against you that the enemy brings. To try and cause distraction to take your mind away from God. But stay focus and keep your mind stayed on God. And he will keep you in perfect peace. Isaiah say Thou wilt keep him in perfect peace, whose mind is stayed on thee: because he trusteth in thee.

# 68

## God Can Help You With The Trials Of Life

The Bible says many are the afflictions of the righteous: but the LORD delivereth him out of them all. So God lets us know that whatever we go through. He will deliver us from all of it. So never fill that you are defeated. It's just a matter of time before you come out of it. It's not if you're coming out. It's when you're coming out. Because you already have the victory.

# God Is A Provider

God will take care of you. He says in Philippians. But my God shall supply all your need according to his riches in glory by Christ Je'-sus. God will take care of all your needs. He says he will supply whatever you need. So you may not have everything you need at that moment. But trust God it's on the way. For God will make a way for you. Because he will supply your every need. He is your provider.

# God Gives Hope

I remember at one time I had no hope. But God sent someone to give me hope. And that's what I'm saying to you. You may not feel there's hope. But God can bring you out. He will bring you thru. No matter what may be wrong in your life. And that's troubling you. God is the only one can help you out. Go to Church. Read his word. Give him your life. And that's your way out.

# God Will Not Leave You

God will not leave you alone. He will always be by your side. You got to trust him even when you can't feel him. He is always by your side even if it may not seem like it. He will show up right on time. You may have a bill due. And you call to get an extension. And it's already paid. You may have a house note behind. And you call and it's paid up for 3 consecutive months. God will not ever abandon you. He will not leave you. Trust him. And he will show you he is still with you.

# Know One Can Love You Like Jesus

Jesus is the only one can love you with real pure love. He has the love that never changes. People may get mad at you for reasons. They may stop coming around you. They may misuse you. They may abuse you. They may do things to cause you pain. And then their feelings change. About loving you. But Jesus will never abuse you. He will love you with a real pure love. No one can love you like Jesus can love you.

# People Are Not God

Don't get mad at God because how people act are do things toward you. People are not God they are man. People may hurt you but remember they are man. So don't stop loving God, are believing in God. Are not wanting to serve God, because how people act. Just remember when they do you wrong. Don't stop loving God. For God will never treat you like man. For God is God and people are man.

# God Still Love You Know Matter What You Have Done

God loves you know matter what you have done. He gives you another chance know matter what you have done. As long as you have breath in you, you have a chance. So don't worry about what you have done. Are where you have been. God forgives and that I know to be true. For if God forgave me of the things I have done. I know he will forgive you. I wasn't always saved. And not any of us was always saved. So remember God forgives if you repent. And ask him to forgive you for your sins. And invite him into your life. Then you can start over and have a brand new life.

# God Loves You So Much

God loves you so much. That he sent his only begotten son Jesus. To redeem us back to him. To give us a right to the tree of life. How many would give there only begotten son to save mankind. Well God did because he loved us just that much. His unconditional love redeem us who want to be saved back to him. Look how much God loves us. What a mighty love he has for us.

## *God Really Cares About You*

God really cares about you. God cares so much Psalm say he collects your tears and put them in a bottle: are they not in thy book. God cares so much he keeps record of every tear you cry. That's real love. Just to be concerned about how many tears you cry.

# God Can Be Your Mother

God can be your mother when you are motherless. He will comfort you in the midnight hours. He will assure you he loves you. You may be going through. And he send someone by just to give you a watermelon. Because he sees you are lonely. He may even send a check in the mail you wasn't expecting just to show you. You're not alone. And he will take care of your needs. God can fill any void you have. Because he is God and beside him there is no other.

# God Can Be Your Father

God can be a father when you are fatherless. You can have something you are trying to put together. And God give you the exacts how to put it together. And you know it was God. You know you couldn't have comprehend it without the wisdom of God. God will be your Father that you are missing. He is Our Father who art in Heaven. He can be your guide even until the end of the world. If you allow him too.

# God Can Be Your Husband

God can be your husband. He can take care of you. You don't have to have a sugar daddy on the side who you know you don't want to be with. You just want what they are giving you. God can take care of you. And you will sleep good at night because you have peace. And you got it the right way. God can be your husband and he will take care of you. If you allow him too.

# *God Can Be Your Wife*

God can be your wife. You don't have to go from one person to another and still not satisfied. After they become common your no longer interested in them. You can wait on God. And let God be all you need him to be. And to be complete in God. Until he sends you a wife. Instead of settling with someone you know you really don't want to be with. And to keep going from person to person.

# Don't Let The Devil Stop You From Praying

You're going to have many tempts from the devil. But don't let him stop you from praying. He want to make you discourage. So you can stop praying. He tries to do things to stop you from praying. But don't let him stop you from praying. For you need prayer and that's true. We can't afford to stop praying. For we need prayer to keep us. So tell the devil leave you alone. For you will always pray. So you can keep winning. Over things that keep coming your way.

# 82

## *Don't Let The Devil Sell You A Counterfeit*

The devil want ever give you the real thing. He will give you silver and not gold. He make it look good on the outside. But he knows what's too it on the inside. So pray about everything you do. Because God will never give you a counterfeit. He will always give you the right thing. He want ever give you nothing that's going to cause you harm, hurt, or danger. He will give you what's best. For he is your Saviour. So don't except the wrong thing. For the devil will never ever give you the right thing.

# 83

## *If You Sow It You're Going To Reap It*

Many people give out things and do things. But when it's there time to go thru things. They act like they can't take things. If you sow it you're going to reap it. And when you do something it's going to come back to you. It may take years it may take months. It may even take days. So remember if you sow it you're going to reap it. And when you're going thru you will remember why you are reaping. For it will come back to your remembrance of what you have done. So remember when you're doing people wrong are even just doing wrong. Remember if you sow it. You are sure enough going to reap it. And that's the word of God.

# 84

## Don't Put Off Being Saved
## Know Longer It's Time

～❋～

It's time to get saved. No pastifying, no putting off it, no sitting in your seat knowing you feel it's time. Time is whining up. Jesus is soon to come back. You know longer need to put off being saved. Jesus can come back any day. So don't put off know longer getting saved. Today is the day you need to except Jesus as your Lord and Saviour. The Bible says if you confess with your mouth and believe in your heart that God raised Jesus from the dead. You are saved. So it's time to get saved. So many souls are dying are you going to be one that die in your sin? For there's a judgment at the end.

## 85

# God Is Not Willing That Any Should Perish

❋

God don't want anyone to leave this world and not be saved. He said he's not willing that any should perish but all should come to repentance. All God want you to do is to repent of your sins. And turn to him. And serve him and you will have eternal life.

# Jesus Is Calling You

When you go to Church and the Pastor is having an altar call for those who want to be saved. And you fill that nudge or pull or feeling he is talking to me. That is Jesus calling you. Your time is now. For you to except Jesus Christ as you Lord and Saviour. Hebews says Today if ye will hear his voice, harden not your hearts, as in the provocation. When you fill that nudge, pull or feeling. Go your time is at hand.

# Jesus Saves

Jesus saves and he wants you to be saved. Jesus came that we might have life and life more abundantly. Jesus came to give us an abundant life. When we live for God. Things will always work out for our good. The good and the bad has to work out for our good because we love God. Jesus wants us to serve him that we will be with him throughout all eternity. That's why God so loved the world that he gave his only begotten son that whosoever believeth in him should not perish, but have everlasting life. Jesus saves and he also wants to save you. So why don't you give him your life.

# 88

## Salvation Is Free

If you believe on the Lord Jesus Christ you can be saved. John says That whosoever believeth in him should not perish, but have eternal life. Salvation is free when you believe. Acts says And they said, Believe on the Lord Je'sus Christ, and thou shalt be saved, and thy house. God not only want to save you but also your house. Salvation is free when you believe.

# Jesus Wants Your Life To Make It Better

Jesus came to give us a right to the tree of life. Jesus came to give us hope. Jesus came to show us love. Jesus came to let us know we don't have to give up on life. Jesus came to redeem us back to God. And if you will allow him to come into your life. Life will get better for you. Because the earth is the Lord and the fullness there of: the world, and they that dwell therein. Jesus came to seek and to save that which was lost.

## Jesus Has Everything You Need

Jesus has everything you need. All you have to do is call upon his holy name. There's nothing too hard for him. Everything belongs to God. He said in Psalm If I were hungry, I would not tell thee: for the world is mine, and the fullness thereof. Everything you need God got it. Jeremiah says The Lord says call unto me, and I will answer thee, and shew thee great and mighty things, which thou knowest not.

# *Jesus Wants To Save You*

Jesus wants to save you. He came to save. John says God sent not his son into the world to condemn the world; but that the world through him might be saved. Jesus purpose for coming was to save. He went to Calvary so that we could be saved. He is the light of the world. And he want to save you. He can and will make a different in your life. If you will give him your life.

# Don't Let The Devil Make You Mess Up Your Walk With God

There's many test you will face and many trials. But all the devil want you to do is mess up with God. See the devil send tempts to make you mess up with God. But don't let what he do make you mess up with God. You may be hurt about something that was done to you. Are even things that disturb you. But don't lose focus on God. Protect your walk with God. And don't let the devil make you mess up your walk with God.

# 93

## Serving The Lord Should Be Serious

———— ❈ ————

Serving the Lord you should take serious. Whatever you do for God it should be sincere. You should take pleasure in serving God. You should be glad you were called. God word says. Many are called, but few are chosen. So you should be thankful. You were the one he chose. So love the Lord, cherish your walk with him. And be thankful you were one he called.

# 94

## Who Are You Serving

You may not say who you are serving. But your lifestyle will let you know. You know were your going and you know what you are doing. So, that let you know who you are serving. It's either the world are it's God. Only what you do for God. It will pay off. Only what you do for Christ will last. So, make sure you are serving God if you want to have eternal life. For only God can give you heaven if you should die.

# 95

## Your Time Is Running Out

Your time is running out. Every year we age. We're getting older. And the choices we make. Determines where we end up in our final destination. If you want to have a victorious ending. The way you live now makes all the difference. When your time has come to the end. Only what we do for Christ will last. That's why we have to put something on our record that will last.

## 96

### Don't Wait Until It's Too Late

Don't wait until it's too late to want to get saved. You may say I'll wait until I am on my death bed to get saved. Who is to say if that was the case you will have a mind to want to get saved? You may fill you have no hope. All hope is lost. What if you have a tragic accident and you don't have time to get saved? What if it's a suddenly and you leave this world? You may not have that time. So don't wait until it's too late. Serve the Lord while the blood is running warm in your veins. Don't wait until it's too late.

# 97

## It Can Be Too Late

Tomorrow is not promise to anyone. There are seasons for everything. You don't know what you may face in this world. You may be okay today. And tomorrow could be a whole another story. But if you have Jesus as your Lord and Saviour already in your life. No matter what happens in your life you will be alright. If you leave this world already serving God. You will be alright. If you leave this world not knowing God. It is too late. When you are dead. It's already over. It's done, it's finish. There are no more chances. It is too late.

# God Can Get You Out Of Trouble

God is the only one can get you out of trouble. You may need a lawyer in court. You may need a doctor to help you out. Whatever trouble you're in. God can bring you out. If you trust God to get you out of trouble. He will bring you out for with God there is always a way out. He wants to help if you let him. He can get you out of trouble if you need help.

# Getting Saved Will Keep You Out Of Trouble

Getting saved will keep you out of trouble. For the word will keep you from having burdens. Things you do when you're not saved, cause you trouble. Because when you don't know God word. That gets you in trouble. People use to say what you don't know it want hurt you. But that's a lie from the pits of hell. The Bible says my people are destroyed for lack of knowledge. So what you don't know. Makes a difference. Because when you do wrong it will cause you to suffer. So get saved today and let God lead you the way. And he will keep you out of trouble. If you will let him protect you from trouble.

# 100

## If You Die Without Jesus You Are In Trouble

If you leave this world without Jesus. You are in serious trouble. There are only two places you can go. Either Heaven or Hell. Jesus says I am the way the truth and the life: no man cometh unto the father, but by me. You can go to heaven only by Jesus. He is the only way. The truth and the life. So don't die without Jesus. For you will be in trouble.

To God the Father, Jesus his son and Precious Holy Spirit. I give God all the Glory for every Book I write. He is the one who has given me great joy. It's an honor to be used by God. And I'm glad he chose me. I Love Jesus for he is my Saviour.

I Love Jesus, God the Father,
And Precious Holy Spirit.
By: Bren Daniels
Jesus The Writer

Printed in the United States
by Baker & Taylor Publisher Services